Grade 5, Book 4

THE HISTORY OF THE MARATHON

CONTENTS

THE RUNNING MESSENGER

In ancient times, there were no telephones or radios. People delivered important messages instead. Messengers travelled by horse or by foot. They often had to run long distances as quickly as possible.

In 490 BC, an army from Persia invaded Greece. The army arrived on the coastal plains of Marathon. This was about 40 kilometres northeast of the city of Athens. An ancient story, or **legend**, tells of a Greek messenger named Pheidippides. He ran from Marathon to Sparta in southern Greece to get help. It is believed that he ran 260 kilometres across rugged country. The long journey took him less than two days.

Location of Marathon

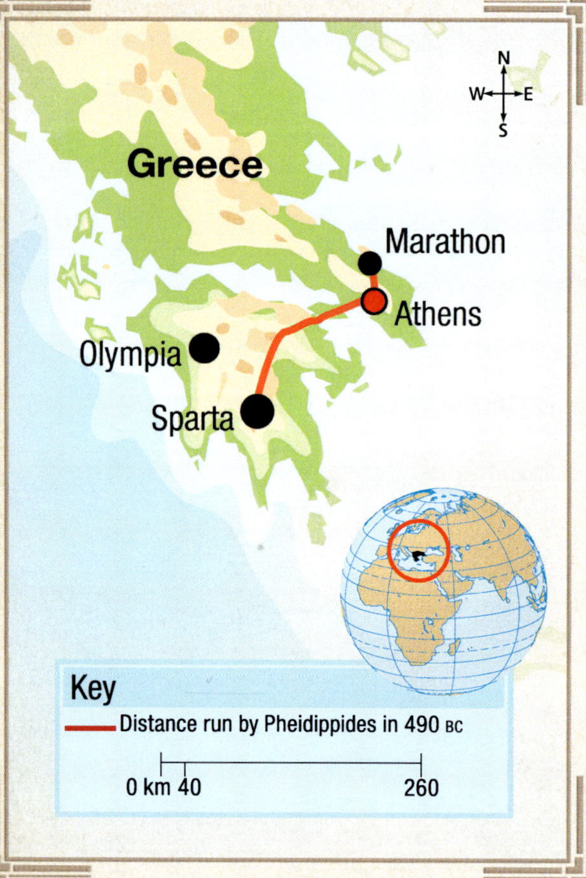

Pheidippides, the Greek messenger

Pheidippides returned with the news that Spartan help would not come for a while. The Athenian army decided not to wait. It attacked and defeated the Persians while they were still preparing for battle. Then, Pheidippides delivered another message. This time, he ran 40 kilometres at top speed from Marathon to Athens. He ran the entire way without stopping. When he reached Athens, he announced the news of the army's victory. Then, he collapsed and died.

It is not known whether this tale is true. However, the legend of Pheidippides' amazing run from Marathon would later inspire the creation of the marathon race.

An artist's impression of the Battle of Marathon, 490 BC

RUNNING CONTESTS

In ancient Greece, exercise and fitness were seen as important. Physical training helped build strong soldiers and armies. In Sparta, boys were trained at military camps from the age of seven. Girls also took part in sports. This was not common in other parts of Greece.

In 776 BC, the first Olympic contest took place in Olympia in western Greece. The whole Games consisted of only one kind of sporting activity, or **event**. It was a running race for male athletes only. The race was 192 metres long. Fifty-two years after this first contest, longer running races were introduced. Later on, other events, such as boxing and chariot racing, also took place. There was even an event in which the athletes taking part, or **contestants**, raced in armour. The contestants usually competed naked.

The ancient Olympic Games were held every four years. Then, in AD 393, Emperor Theodosius I banned the Games.

In the 1850s, a wealthy Greek man revived the Olympic Games. His name was Evangelis Zappas. The Games took place in Athens. The events included running races, javelin, discus and wrestling. The winners were given cash, medals and olive branches. Zappas died in 1865. He left money in his will to fund future Games. The Greek government held the Games in 1870, 1875 and 1888. These Games were not very well organised. They were also not very successful.

Ancient Greeks racing chariots at Olympia

THE MARATHON VISION

The Games did, however, catch the attention of a French nobleman and educator. His name was Baron Pierre de Coubertin. In 1875, German archaeologists had uncovered ruins at Olympia. They had found the ancient stadium and temples. The ruins inspired de Coubertin. He wanted to revive the Olympic Games. He believed that physical exercise was important. He also felt that a friendly sporting competition between nations would be a good thing. It would bring them closer together.

In 1894, de Coubertin hosted an international meeting. Sportsmen from 79 countries attended. He put forward his idea of reviving the Olympic Games. The International Athletic Conference was formed. It later became the International Olympic Committee (IOC). The IOC hoped to stage the first modern Olympic Games in the ancient city of Athens.

Baron Pierre de Coubertin (1863-1937), founder of the modern Olympic Games

The first Olympic organising committee, Athens, Greece, 1896

De Coubertin and the IOC wanted to include a showcase event in the first modern Games. They wanted something that linked it to ancient Greece. It was to be an event to catch the attention of the world.

It was Michel Bréal, a friend of de Coubertin's, who suggested a new long-distance race. Bréal was a French scholar. He was fascinated by the legend of Pheidippides. He believed that a race from Marathon to Athens would be a good idea. It would link the modern Olympic Games to ancient Greece.

De Coubertin and the IOC liked the idea. Then, de Coubertin visited Athens to see if Greece would host the race. The Greek government was very excited about the plan.

THE FIRST MARATHON

The date had finally arrived. On 6 April 1896, the first modern Olympic Games began. There were 311 athletes from 14 nations. There were nine different sporting events. The Greek team consisted of 230 male athletes.

The new long-distance race would be the highlight. It would take place on the last day of the five-day sporting event. The planned course started at a bridge in the village of Marathon. It ended in the stadium in Athens. The distance was 40 kilometres. The course went over mountains, valleys and dusty roads. The race, of course, would be called the marathon.

The Greek government very much wanted a Greek contestant to win the first marathon. Before race day, they held two practice, or **trial**, races. These would help them select who would represent their country. On 10 March 1896, 12 runners ran from Marathon to Athens. The contestants were all from sports clubs in Greece. Charilaos Vasilakos won the first race.

On 24 March 1896, a second trial race took place. This time, 38 runners lined up at the start. This race was open to non-club runners. A water carrier named Spiridon Louis finished fifth. However, he also qualified to run in the first Olympic marathon. His time was the same as the winner of the first trial race.

The start of the men's 100-metre race at the 1896 Olympic Games in Athens, Greece, won by Tom Burke of the US

THE BIG DAY

On 10 April 1896, 17 competitors took part in the first modern marathon race. There were only four foreign runners. The Greek competitors were the only ones who had run the course before.

One entrant, Australian Edwin Flack, had already won gold medals. He had won the 800-metre and 1,500-metre Olympic races. Arthur Blake was the runner from the United States. He had finished second in the 1,500-metre race. Albin Lermusiaux represented France. Gyula Kellner was from Hungary. He was the only foreign runner who had run such a long distance before. Italian Carlo Airoldi was excluded from the competition, or **disqualified**. Like today, the Olympic Games were open only to non-professional, or **amateur**, athletes. Airoldi had run professionally before. He did not count as an amateur. Sadly, his 1,500-kilometre journey by foot to get to the Games from Italy had been wasted.

Edwin Flack, Australia, gold medal winner

The race was to start in the village of Marathon. Here, several hundred spectators were eagerly waiting. Thousands of spectators filled the stadium in Athens. This was where the race would finish. Many more lined the road leading to the stadium. At 2 p.m., the race was going to begin. After a long speech, a starting pistol fired. The athletes took off at a fast pace. Helpers in charge of the race, or **officials**, and doctors followed the runners along the course. They used bicycles and horse-drawn wagons.

The Olympic Stadium in Athens
at the first modern Olympic Games in 1896

The French runner, Lermusiaux, took the lead early. The village of Pikermi was just past the halfway mark. By the time Lermusiaux reached this village, the closest competitors were about 3 kilometres behind him. At this stage in the race, none of those runners were from Greece. The leaders were Flack, Blake and Kellner. Spiridon Louis arrived at Pikermi well back from the leaders. Amazingly, he stopped for a glass of wine and then continued running.

The second half of the race included much uphill running. The runners would need a lot of energy for this. However, the early leaders had used up much of their strength. They had run too fast too soon. They began to slow down. The Greek runners began to catch up.

Three participants in the first marathon race in a modern Olympic Games

Blake, the American runner, was the first to drop out of the race. He was exhausted. Then, Lermusiaux collapsed. He rode the rest of the way to the stadium on a cart. After that, Kellner began to slow down. The Greek runners, led by Spiridon Louis, soon overtook him.

With the race almost over, Flack was still in the lead. He was one of only two foreign runners left in the race. However, Louis was catching up. He put on a burst of speed and then passed the Australian. Flack tried to match his speed. He stumbled and fell. He had to be carried off.

Spiridon Louis (1873-1940)

A messenger on horseback brought the good news to the crowd at the stadium. Louis was in the lead. About 100,000 people, including the Greek royal family, were eagerly awaiting him. On the way to the stadium, Louis even felt he had time to stop to eat slices of orange.

Then, he ran into the stadium. Crown Prince Nicholas and Prince George waited there for him. When Louis ran in, they ran alongside him to the finish line. The crowd went wild. Louis was a national hero.

Spiridon Louis completed the race in 2 hours, 58 minutes and 50 seconds. About seven minutes later, the second runner crossed the finish line. It was Greek contestant Charilaos Vasilakos. He had won the first trial race. Then, in third place came Spiridon Belokas. Kellner, the Hungarian, came fourth. After the race, Kellner complained, or made a **protest**. He claimed Belokas had travelled part of the way in a carriage. Belokas admitted it was true. The race officials disqualified him. Kellner was awarded third place.

Spiridon Louis entering the stadium with Crown Prince Nicholas and Prince George

Two sides of the Olympic medal from the 1896 Games in Athens

Five days later, the victorious Louis had his prize-giving ceremony. He was given a silver cup, a silver medal and an olive branch. Today, of course, Olympic first-place winners get gold medals, not silver ones.

Since this exciting beginning, the marathon has become a regular race at the Olympic Games. The American team returned home full of excitement about the first marathon. The following year, America held a marathon in Boston. The Boston Marathon has taken place every year since 1897.

The silver cup awarded at the 1896 marathon

The King of Greece, Georgios I, presenting awards at the first Olympic Games

A MEMORABLE MARATHON

The 1908 Olympic marathon was very exciting and had a dramatic finish, too. One spectator even described it as 'the greatest race of the century'.

The 1908 Olympic Games were held in London, England. The marathon began at 2.33 p.m. on 24 July. It was a hot, humid day. Italian runner Dorando Pietri began slowly. In the second half of the race, he put on a burst of speed that took him to the lead. However, it was all too much. By the time he entered the stadium, he was weak from fatigue and dehydration. He ran the wrong way. The officials redirected him, but he fell down. The officials helped him up. He staggered on. Then, he fell again. He fell four more times. Each time, the officials helped him up.

Dorando Pietri finishing the Olympic marathon in London, 1908

Finally, Pietri crossed the finish line in first place. He ran 42.195 kilometres in 2 hours, 54 minutes and 46 seconds. The last 350 metres took him 10 minutes! American runner Johnny Hayes crossed the line in second place. The American team filed a protest. They said that Pietri would not have finished the race without help. The protest was upheld. Pietri was disqualified. Hayes was declared the winner. However, Pietri became a hero to his country and the world. The marathon also received worldwide attention.

Johnny Hayes winning the marathon race, Olympic Games, London, 1908

GOING THE DISTANCE

When the marathon was first created, there was no exact set distance. The distance run by the legendary Pheidippides was about 40 kilometres. The only rule was that a marathon had to be about this length. So, each time the race was run, the distance was a little different. It all depended on the route. Here are the distances for the first seven Olympic marathons. (In 1916, during World War I, the Olympic Games were not held.)

Distances for the First Seven Olympic Marathons

Distance	(40 km)	(40.26 km)	(40 km
Year	1896	1890	1904
City	Athens	Paris	St Louis
Country	Greece	France	United States

In 1921, the International Amateur Athletic Federation (IAAF) set a standard distance for the marathon. It looked back to the 1908 Olympic marathon in London and used that distance – 42.195 kilometres. No one really knows why they chose this particular marathon. Perhaps it was because the 1908 Olympic marathon was so memorable.

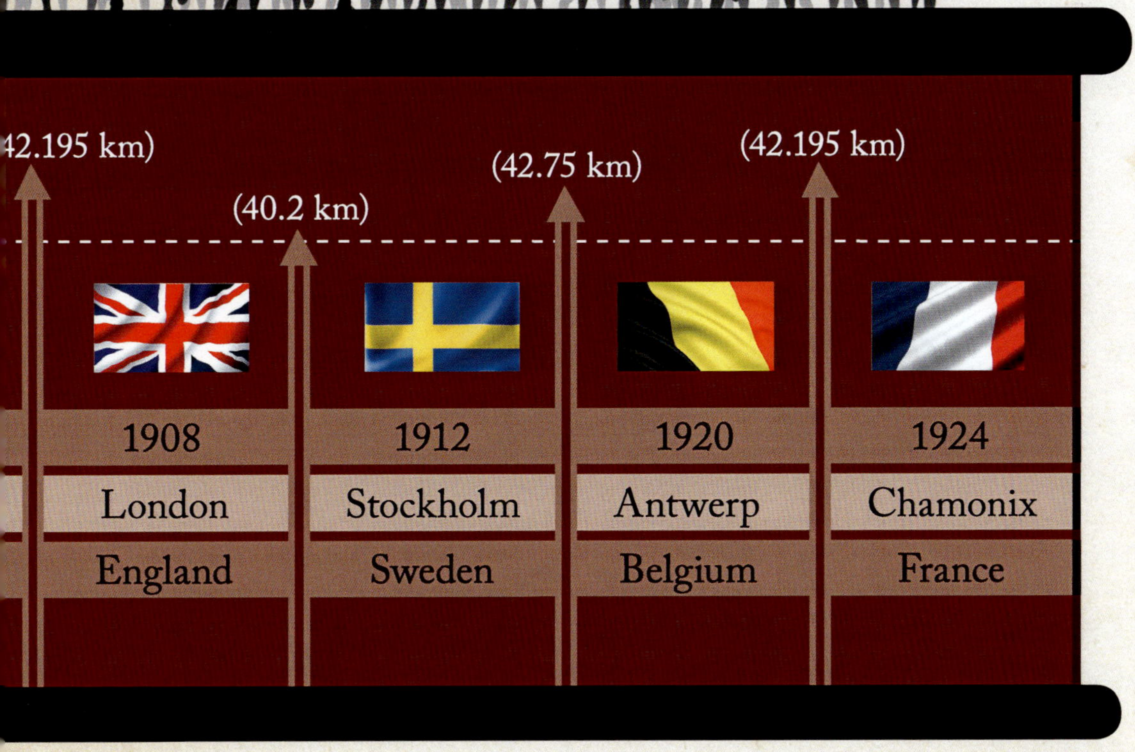

THE WORLD'S GREATEST RACE

When the Olympic Games began, only men were allowed to compete. In 1900, female athletes were able to participate for the first time. It took another 84 years before the Olympic Games held its first women's marathon.

Today, every year, more than 800 marathons take place all over the world. There are races for amateurs and professionals. Some of these races have up to 30,000 competitors. Some marathon courses are in unusual places. They take place on the Great Wall of China. They take place across African safari parks. There are even races on Greenland's freezing ice cap. For the runners taking part, there is no greater race on Earth.

Wilma Rudolph breaks the tape at the finish line to win a gold medal for the women's 4 x 100 metres at the 1960 Olympic Games, Rome, Italy.

GLOSSARY

amateur – a person who takes part in an activity for pleasure, rather than money

contestants – people taking part in a race or event

disqualified – when someone is prevented from taking part in an activity or a sporting event, usually because the person has broken a rule

event – a race or other competition that forms part of a larger sports occasion

legend – a story from the past. Legends are often based on fact, but they are not always true.

officials – helpers at an event who enforce the rules and look after contestants

protest – to object to something that a person has done or said

trial – a practice run to see who should compete in the final event

INDEX

Activities

Genre Focus

Historical Recount

A historical recount records a series of factual events, from some time in history, in the order in which they occurred.

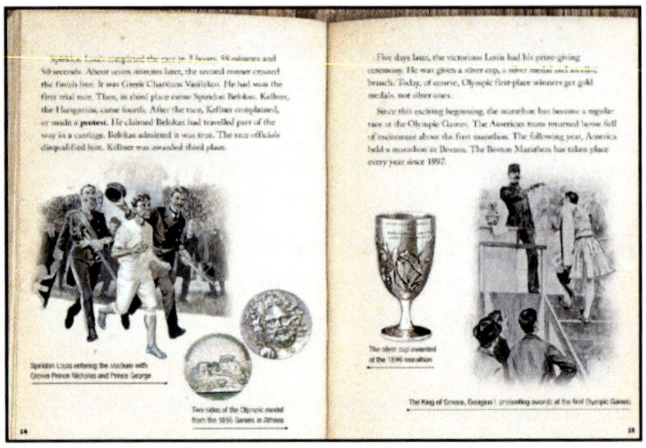

Looking back at a HISTORICAL RECOUNT

This book is about early running competitions, the idea for the Olympic marathon and the running of the event throughout history.

1. A historical recount begins with an orientation. In this book, pages 2 and 3 introduce the text by recounting the run of a Greek messenger named Pheidippides.

   a) How far did Pheidippides run when Persia invaded Greece?
   b) What happened at the end of Pheidippides' run to Athens?

2. The next chapters give an ordered account of the development of the Olympic marathon and marathon running around the world. Draw up and complete a chart like the one below to record the main idea for each paragraph in the chapter *The Big Day*. You will need 12 boxes for the 12 paragraphs.

Paragraph 1: On 10 April, 17 competitors took part in the first modern marathon race.
↓
Paragraph 2:

3. A feature of historical recounts is time connectives – words and phrases that indicate time. Go back through the text and locate and list all the time-related words that indicate when something occurred, for example *in ancient times, this time, finally.*

Writing a Historical Recount

You are going to write a historical recount that is based around the Olympic Games. The topic of your recount is *The Ancient Olympics*. You will need to use a variety of resources to read and take notes that will help you write your text.

1. Begin by writing an orientation. Answering this question will help you to introduce your topic: What were the ancient Olympics?

2. Now, use your notes to help you write a series of events about the ancient Olympic Games in the order in which they occurred. Consider the following questions as you write: When were the first recorded ancient Olympic Games? Where were they held? Who participated in them? What were the original events and what events were added? When and why did the ancient Olympic Games cease?

3. Round off your recount by making a statement about the gap in time between the ancient Olympics and the modern Olympics.

4. Read back through your text to see if you have presented your information in the past tense. Make sure your information is factual. Check that you have used time connectives to sequence your events.

Comprehension Focus

Sequencing

Remember

Sequencing is the arranging of actions, events or instructions in the order in which they occur/occurred.

1. You are going to make pieces for a game called *Olympics in Sequence*. To do this you need to go back through *The History of the Marathon* and record all the dates and what happened at that particular time. These are examples: 490 BC, Pheidippides ran from Marathon to Sparta; 776 BC, the first Olympic contest took place in Olympia; 1900, Olympic Games held in Paris, France. (Don't forget the chart on page 18.) You may need to write the same event for a number of dates, for example, the Greek government held Games in 1870, 1875 and 1888 (page 5).
2. When you have taken these notes, write each of the events on a separate strip of paper (not the dates).
3. Rule up a two-column chart. Down the left-hand column, list all the dates in order.
4. Jumble up your paper strips of events. Watch the clock and time how long it takes you to complete the second column by ordering your paper strips to match the dates.
5. Ask friends to complete the activity to see who is quickest to correctly order the events.